KINGFISHER READERS

Bears

Thea Feldman

KINGFISHER

First published 2017 by Kingfisher
an imprint of Macmillan Children's Books
20 New Wharf Road, London N1 9RR
Associated companies throughout the world
www.panmacmillan.com

Series editor: Hayley Down
Literacy consultant: Hilary Horton
Design: Peter Clayman

ISBN 978-0-7534-4093-3

9 8 7 6 5 4 3 2

2TR/1117/WKT/UG/105MA

A CIP catalogue record for this book is available from the British Library.

Printed in China

Picture credits

The Publisher would like to thank the following for permission to reproduce their material.
Top = t; Bottom = b; Centre = c; Left = l; Right = r
Cover iStock/Marc_Latremouille; Pages 3 iStock/Dieter Meyrl; 4–5 Shutterstock/ArCaLu; 6
iStock/David Hughes; 7 iStock/Sandra vom Stein; 8 iStock/webguzs; 9 Alamy/Wayne Lynch; 10
FLPA/Imagebroker; 11 Getty/Auscape/UIG; 12 iStock/leungchopan; 13 Alamy/WILDLIFE GmbH;
14 Shutterstock/kunanon; 15 FLPA/Imagebroker; 16 Alamy/Arco Images GmbH; 17 Alamy/
Edward Parker; 18 iStock/chaney1; 19 Getty/Don Johnston; 20 Alamy/Ganesh H Shankar; 21,
22–23 FLPA/Sylvain Cordier/Biosphoto; 24 Getty/Katherine Feng; 26 Alamy/Ron Niebrugge; 27
iStock/LuCaAr; 28 iStock/Justinreznick; 29 iStock/ErikMandre; 30 Alamy/All Canada Photos; 31
iStock/Dieter Meyrl.

Hello, bear!

This is a brown bear.

She was asleep in a cave all winter.

Now it is spring.

The brown bear comes outside.

The bear stands on her hind legs.

She sniffs the air to find food.

Brown bears eat fruit,
insects, plants and fish.

This brown bear catches a fish
with his teeth!

There are eight kinds of bear.

The polar bear is the largest bea

Polar bears live in the **Arctic**.

The Arctic is a very cold place.

A polar bear hunts for
seals on floating ice.

The sun bear is the smallest bear.

The sun bear lives
in a warm **forest**.

The sun bear has a very long tongue. He uses his tongue to reach honey and bees deep inside beehives.

Munch, munch, munch!

The panda bear eats
mostly **bamboo**.

All pandas are black and white. But each panda looks different from all the rest!

Look at the **fur** on this bear.

The pale fur on her chest
is shaped like a moon.

That is why she is called
a moon bear!

The sun bear is named
for the fur on his chest too.

Does the fur look like
the sun to you?

This is the spectacled bear.

The circles around her
eyes look like **spectacles**.

The spectacled bear is very good at climbing trees.

She builds a nest high up in the tree.

The spectacled bear eats and sleeps in the nest.

This black bear uses her sharp claws to climb a tree.

She looks in the tree for fruit.

A sloth bear rests on
a tree branch.

Would you like to rest there?

A sloth bear has long, thick fur.

Baby sloth bears hold onto the fur on their mother's back to take a ride!

A baby bear is called a **cub**.

Most bears have two cubs
at the same time.

A **newborn** cub is tiny.

A baby panda weighs about 85 grams.

He is about the size of a lemon.

A panda will weigh more than 90 kilograms when he grows up!

This cub is three weeks old.

Most bear cubs are born without fur.

They cannot see or hear when they are born.

Cubs start to see and hear when they are about one month old.

Bear cubs stay close to their mother for the first few months of their life.

A mother bear teaches
her cubs many things.

One day they will live
on their own.

Some bear cubs are born when their mother is in a **den**.

The cubs drink their mother's milk and grow in the den.

They stay safe there until spring.

Then they come outside for the first time.

Hello, bear … and cub!

Glossary

Arctic the area that is the farthest north on the Earth, it includes the Arctic Ocean and parts of Europe, Asia and North America

bamboo a tall, thick, tough grass that is the main food of pandas

cub the name given to some baby animals, including baby bears

den a cave or nest where a bear lives

forest a large piece of land that is covered with trees and other plants

fur the soft hair that covers many animals

newborn an animal that has just been born

spectacles a pair of glasses